Facilitator's Guide

The Reflective Educator's Guide to Classroom Research

Learning to Teach and Teaching to Learn Through Practitioner Inquiry

NANCY FICHTMAN DANA   DIANE YENDOL-HOPPEY

SECOND EDITION

CORWIN PRESS
A SAGE Company

For information:

Corwin Press
A SAGE Company
2455 Teller Road
Thousand Oaks, California 91320
www.corwinpress.com

SAGE Ltd.
1 Oliver's Yard
55 City Road
London EC1Y 1SP
United Kingdom

SAGE India Pvt. Ltd.
B 1/I 1 Mohan Cooperative Industrial Area
Mathura Road, New Delhi 110 044
India

SAGE Asia-Pacific Pte. Ltd.
33 Pekin Street #02-01
Far East Square
Singapore 048763

Printed in the United States of America

ISBN: 978-1-4129-6654-2

This book is printed on acid-free paper.

08   09   10   11   12   10   9   8   7   6   5   4   3   2   1

Acquisitions Editor:	Carol Chambers Collins
Editorial Assistant:	Brett Ory
Production Editor:	Melanie Birdsall
Copy Editor:	Bill Bowers
Typesetter:	C&M Digitals (P) Ltd.
Proofreader:	Dorothy Hoffman
Cover Designer:	Michael Dubowe

Contents

About the Authors

Nancy Fichtman Dana is currently a Professor of Education and Director of the Center for School Improvement at the University of Florida (http://education.ufl.edu/csi). Under her direction, the Center promotes and supports practitioner inquiry as a core mechanism for school improvement in schools throughout the state. Prior to her appointment at the University of Florida, she served on the faculty of Curriculum and Instruction at The Pennsylvania State University, where she developed and directed the State College Area School District–Pennsylvania State University Elementary Professional Development School program, named the 2002 Distinguished Program in Teacher Education by the Association of Teacher Educators, and the 2004 Zimpher Best Partnership by the National Holmes Partnership. Nancy holds a PhD in Elementary Education from Florida State University. She began her career in education as an elementary school teacher in Hannibal Central Schools, New York, and has worked closely with elementary school teachers on teacher inquiry and school-university collaborations in Florida and Pennsylvania since 1990. She has authored two other books with Diane Yendol-Hoppey: *The Reflective Educator's Guide to Professional Development: Coaching Inquiry-Oriented Learning Communities* and *The Reflective Educator's Guide to Mentoring: Strengthening Practice Through Knowledge, Story, and Metaphor,* as well as numerous articles in professional journals focused on teacher inquiry, teacher leadership, school-university collaborations, and professional development schools.

Diane Yendol-Hoppey is currently Professor of Education and Director of the Benedum Collaborative at West Virginia University. Prior to her appointment at West Virginia University, she served as the Coordinator of the Elementary Apprenticeship, Director of the Northeast Florida Teachers' Network Leadership Institute and evaluator of numerous district, state, and national professional development efforts at University o Florida. Before beginning her work in higher education, Diane spent 13 years as an elementary school teacher in Pennsylvania and Maryland. She holds a PhD in Curriculum and Instruction from The Pennsylvania State University. Diane's current work focuses on developing school-university partnerships committed to cultivating an inquiry stance and a commitment to teacher leadership. Diane received the American Educational Research Association (AERA) Division K Early Career Research Award for her ongoing commitment to researching innovative approaches to professional development. She has authored articles in professional journals focusing on creating communities of inquiry, teacher leadership, mentoring, and school-university collaboration, as well as three books with Nancy Fichtman Dana.

Introduction

How to Use This Guide

This facilitator's guide is a companion to *The Reflective Educator's Guide to Classroom Research: Learning to Teach and Teaching to Learn Through Practitioner Inquiry*, Second Edition, by Nancy Fichtman Dana and Diane Yendol-Hoppey. It is designed to accompany the study of the book and provide assistance to group facilitators, such as school leaders, professional development coordinators, peer coaches, team leaders, mentors, and professors. Along with a summary of each chapter in the book, Nancy Fichtman Dana and Diane Yendol-Hoppey have provided chapter discussion questions, activities, journal writing prompts, and resources for extending learning.

When using the guide during independent study, focus on the summaries and discussion questions. For small study groups, the facilitator should guide the group through the chapter work. For small or large group workshops, the facilitator should create an agenda by selecting activities and discussion starters from the chapter reviews that meet the group's goals, and guide the group through the learning process.

After the chapter summaries and recommendations for activities found throughout the Chapter-by-Chapter Study Guide, we have suggested a series of two- to three-hour workshop agendas distributed over an entire school year (September–May) that we have found to be the most powerful way to utilize this book to guide teachers through the inquiry process step-by-step. Note that the suggested timeframe of these workshops can be condensed to start at any time in the school year or to fit within a typical 16-week semester, if you are utilizing this book as a required text for a college course on action research. For example, we have used this book and covered its entire contents effectively beginning in January and ending in May, and we have also used this book effectively by beginning late in a school year or during the summer months and using the book to help teachers plan an inquiry they wish to engage in during the following school year. However you use this book, we have learned that the quality of teachers' research is directly related to the quality of the coaching the teachers receive in the process. This facilitator's guide is designed to support those in roles that coach teacher action research. For additional support and ideas for helping teachers through each phase of the inquiry process, you may also be interested in *The Reflective Educator's Guide to Professional Development: Coaching Inquiry-Oriented Learning Communities*, a companion book we wrote to this text. That volume offers the reader multiple stories of action research coaches and facilitators and the ways they helped teachers cultivate their first wonderings, design a plan for inquiry, analyze data, and share their learning with others.

Additional Resources for Facilitators

Corwin Press also offers a free 16-page resource titled *Tips for Facilitators*, which includes practical strategies and tips for guiding a successful meeting. The information in this section describes different professional development opportunities, the principles of effective professional development, some characteristics of an effective facilitator, the responsibilities of the facilitator, and practical tips and strategies to make the meeting more successful. *Tips for Facilitators* is available for free download at the Corwin Press Web site (www.corwinpress.com, under "Resources/Tips for Facilitators").

We recommend that facilitators download a copy of *Tips for Facilitators* and review the characteristics and responsibilities of facilitators and professional development strategies for different types of work groups and settings.

Chapter-by-Chapter Study Guide

The Reflective Educator's Guide to Classroom Research: Learning to Teach and Teaching to Learn Through Practitioner Inquiry, Second Edition

by Nancy Fichtman Dana
and Diane Yendol-Hoppey

Chapter 1. Teacher Inquiry Defined

Summary

This chapter begins by providing an overview of the teacher inquiry process that includes a history of the teacher inquiry movement. Three educational research traditions are described, compared, and contrasted to one another: the process-product paradigm, the qualitative or interpretive paradigm, and the teacher inquiry paradigm. Through comparison of these research traditions, it is concluded that, "While both the process-product and qualitative research paradigms have generated valuable insights into the teaching and learning process, they have not included the voices of the people closest to the children—classroom teachers." Hence, the critical importance of the teacher inquiry movement as raising teachers' voices in discussions of educational reform is established.

Following this brief overview of the history of educational research, inquiry is defined as systematic, intentional study by teachers of their own teaching practice. Inquiring professionals seek out change by reflecting on their practice. They do this by posing questions or "wonderings," collecting data to gain insights into their wonderings, analyzing the data along with reading relevant literature, making changes in practice based on new understandings developed during inquiry, and sharing findings with others. This process offers a fresh approach to teacher professional development.

To help teachers tie the inquiry process to current and related trends in teacher professional development, the relationships between inquiry and differentiated instruction, data-driven decision making and progress monitoring, and Response to Intervention are discussed. These discussions help readers connect inquiry to other current initiatives and make inquiry a part of, rather than apart from, their work as reflective classroom teachers. Yet, two differences between being a reflective classroom teacher and a teacher-inquirer are noted: (1) Teacher inquiry is less happenstance; and (2) teacher inquiry is more visible.

The chapter concludes by describing three contexts that are ripe for teacher inquiry: professional learning communities, student teaching and/or other clinical experiences, and professional development schools and other teacher networks.

Discussion Questions

1. What role does teacher inquiry play in educational reform?
2. The authors state, "Teacher inquiry is a vehicle that can be used by teachers to untangle some of the complexity that occurs in the profession, raise teachers' voices in discussions of educational reform, and ultimately transform assumptions about the teaching profession itself." What are some common assumptions the general public holds about teaching and learning that you would like to see challenged? How can your engagement in inquiry help to challenge these assumptions?
3. What conceptions about educational research did you hold prior to beginning this book? To articulate your prior conceptions, consider the following:
   - Who does educational research?
   - Where is educational research done?
   - When is educational research done?
   - Why is educational research done?
   - How is educational research done?
   - What do you see as the strengths and weaknesses of educational research?
   - Do you think that practitioners value educational research? Why or why not?

- Is there anything missing from educational research as you see it?
- In what ways might engagement in teacher inquiry address what is missing?

4. How does engagement in teacher inquiry differ from traditional models of professional development?

5. Which ripe contexts for teacher inquiry (professional learning communities, student teaching and/or other clinical experiences, professional development schools, and other teacher networks) are most pertinent to your current position? How can/will engagement in inquiry become a part of your current work as an educator?

6. What excites you about the teacher inquiry movement? What concerns you?

7. How do you feel about embarking on your personal teacher inquiry journey?

Activities

Activity 1.1: Block Party

This activity was adapted from a protocol titled Block Party, *adapted by Debbie Bambino from Kylene Beers's prereading strategy from the National School Reform Faculty Web site. Please visit their Web site (www.nsrfharmony.org) for additional text-based protocols that can be utilized to discuss this chapter.*

Time: 30 minutes
Materials: Handout 1: Twelve Interesting Quotes From Chapter 1

Step 1: Copy and cut apart the quotes in Handout 1: Twelve Interesting Quotes From Chapter 1 so that each participant will receive one quote. You may wish to glue each quote on an index card to make them easier for participants to handle. If you are working with more than 12 people, quotes may be repeated.

Step 2: Have each participant randomly select one quote. Once each person has received a quote, ask them to flip the quote over and write a statement about what this quote means to them. (5 minutes)

Step 3: Participants get up and mingle to find a partner who received a different quote from the one they received. Once everyone has a partner, state that each pair should share their quotes with their partners, as well as what each quote meant to them. (5 minutes)

Step 4: Repeat Step 3 two more times with a different partner. (10 minutes)

Step 5: Participants return to their seats. Facilitator leads whole group in a discussion of ideas and questions about teacher inquiry raised by this experience. (10 minutes)

● *Activity 1.2: Save the Last Word for Me*

This activity, developed by Patricia Averette, was adapted from the protocol Save the Last Word for Me, *from the National School Reform Faculty Web site. Please visit their Web site (www.nsrfharmony.org) for additional text-based protocols that can be utilized to discuss this chapter.*

Time: 30 minutes
Materials: *The Reflective Educator's Guide to Classroom Research: Learning to Teach and Teaching to Learn Through Practitioner Inquiry,* Second Edition, one highlighter for each participant

Step 1: Create groups of four participants. Ask the person in the group with the closest birthday to today's date to serve in the role of timekeeper. The timekeeper must either have a watch or borrow a watch from another member of the group. The timekeeper also participates.

Step 2: Ask each person to open up *The Reflective Educator's Guide to Classroom Research: Learning to Teach and Teaching to Learn Through Practitioner Inquiry* (Second Edition) to Chapter 1. Silently, each person skims Chapter 1 to find what he or she feels to be the most significant idea addressed in the chapter, and highlights that passage.

Step 3: When the group is ready, the person in the group whose last name comes first alphabetically begins by identifying the part of Chapter 1 that he or she found to be the most significant and reads it out loud to the group. The person (the presenter) says nothing about why he or she chose that particular passage.

Step 4: The other three participants each have 1 minute to respond to the passage—saying what it makes them think about, and what questions the passage raised for them about teacher inquiry.

Step 5: The first participant then has 3 minutes to state why he or she chose that part of Chapter 1 and to respond to—or build on—what he or she heard from his or her colleagues.

Step 6: The same pattern is followed until all four members of the group have had a chance to be the presenter and to have "the last word."

Step 7 (Optional): Facilitate a whole-group discussion about Chapter 1 and the ideas and questions raised in the individual groups of four during the first six steps of this activity.

Journal Writing Prompt

One word that describes how I feel about conducting my own personal inquiry into my teaching practice this school year is _____. I chose this word because _____

_____

_____

_____.

Resources for Extending Your Learning

The following books and resources are collections of teacher research and include many rich examples of what teacher research might look like. Examples of teacher research provide a nice complement to Chapter 1:

Caro-Bruce, C., Flessner, R., Klehr, M., & Zeichner, K. M. (2007). *Creating equitable classrooms through action research.* Thousand Oaks, CA: Corwin Press.

Center for School Improvement Web site at the University of Florida. (http://education.ufl.edu/csi)

Masingila, J. O. (2006). *Teachers engaged in research: Inquiry into mathematics classrooms.* Greenwich, CT: Information Age Publishing.

Meyers, E., & Rust, F. (Eds.). (2003). *Taking action with teacher research.* Portsmouth, NH: Heinemann.

The following books provide the theoretical foundation for teacher inquiry:

Carr, W., & Kemmis, S. (1986). *Becoming critical: Education, knowledge, and action research.* Geelong, Victoria, Australia: Deakin University Press.

Cochran-Smith, M., & Lytle, S. L. (1993). *Inside/outside: Teacher research and knowledge.* New York: Teachers College Press.

Chapter 2. The Start of Your Journey: Finding a Wondering

Summary

This chapter guides readers through the first step in the teacher inquiry process—developing a "wondering." A wondering is defined as a burning question a teacher has about his or her classroom practice that emerges from that teacher's daily work in the classroom and his or her teaching dilemmas or "felt difficulties."

Eight passions are named as ripe places for teachers to formulate a wondering. These passions include:

1. A Child
2. Curriculum
3. Content Knowledge
4. Teaching Strategies/Techniques
5. Beliefs About Practice
6. The Intersection of Your Personal and Professional Identities
7. Advocating Social Justice
8. Context

Each passion is illustrated with the work of prospective and practicing teacher-inquirers, and analyzes the thought processes these inquirers utilized to derive their first wonderings. A series of exercises also accompanies each passion to help teachers explore potential wonderings.

(*Note to facilitator:* Facilitators should consider having their participants read pages 165–175 of Chapter 7, which introduces the importance of quality and focuses on assessing the quality of teacher research at the same time as they read this chapter. By using both chapters together, the "developing a wondering" process can be strengthened.)

Discussion Questions

1. What are some common real-world dilemmas teachers face each day? What types of questions do these dilemmas raise?
2. Which of the eight passions (A Child, Curriculum, Content Knowledge, Teaching Strategies/Techniques, Beliefs About Practice, The Intersection of Personal and Professional Identities, Advocating Social Justice, and Context) do you feel is *most* important to explore at this time in your professional lifetime? Why?
3. Which of the eight passions (A Child, Curriculum, Content Knowledge, Teaching Strategies/Techniques, Beliefs About Practice, The Intersection of Personal and Professional Identities, Advocating Social Justice, and Context) do you feel is *least* important to explore at this point in your professional lifetime? Why?
4. How could the contents of Chapter 7 strengthen our ability to engage in developing a wondering?

Activities

● *Activity 2.1: The Great Wondering Brainstorm*

Time: 30–45 minutes
Materials: Handout 2: The Great Wondering Brainstorm

Step 1: Briefly review each of the eight passions described in Chapter 2 of *The Reflective Educator's Guide to Classroom Research:*

Learning to Teach and Teaching to Learn Through Practitioner Inquiry (Second Edition). (5–10 minutes)

Step 2: Distribute one copy of Handout 2: The Great Wondering Brainstorm to each participant. Ask participants to list one or two wonderings they have about their practice in relationship to each passion. (10 minutes)

Step 3: Ask participants to review their list of wonderings and place stars next to the top three wonderings on their list that they feel would be most important for them to explore through the process of inquiry this school year. (5 minutes)

Step 4: Participants share their top three wonderings with the person next to them, sharing the wondering itself as well as their reasoning for selecting that wondering as one of their top three choices for exploration through the process of inquiry. (10 minutes)

Step 5: Facilitator leads a whole-group discussion asking participants to share what they learned about themselves and/or their colleagues by participating in the great wondering brainstorm. (10–15 minutes)

● *Activity 2.2: Passion Jigsaw*

This activity is a great way to cover the contents of Chapter 2 if your participants have not read the chapter prior to your meeting or workshop. It works best if there are at least eight people in your group.

Time: 90 minutes
Materials: One copy of *The Reflective Educator's Guide to Classroom Research: Learning to Teach and Teaching to Learn Through Practitioner Inquiry* (Second Edition) for each participant

Step 1: Have the participants in your workshop count off by eights (1, 2, 3, 4, 5, 6, 7, 8, 1, 2, 3, 4, 5, 6, 7, 8, 1, 2, and so on). Assign each "number" a corresponding passion to read in Chapter 2 of *The Reflective Educator's Guide to Classroom Research* (Second Edition):
  • Ones—Read Passion 1: Helping an Individual Child (pp. 22–29)
  • Twos—Read Passion 2: Desire to Improve or Enrich Curriculum (pp. 29–33)
  • Threes—Read Passion 3: Focus on Developing Content Knowledge (pp. 34–36)
  • Fours—Read Passion 4: Desire to Improve or Experiment With Teaching Strategies and Teaching Techniques (pp. 36–38)
  • Fives—Read Passion 5: Desire to Explore the Relationship Between Your Beliefs and Your Classroom Practice (pp. 38–40)

- Sixes—Read Passion 6: The Intersection of Your Personal and Professional Identities (pp. 40–46)
- Sevens—Read Passion 7: Advocating Social Justice (pp. 47–54)
- Eights—Read Passion 8: Focus on Understanding the Teaching and Learning Context (pp. 54–55)

As participants read, ask them to jot down some notes about their passion, as they will be responsible for teaching others about their passion later in the activity. (10–15 minutes)

Step 2: Create "expert" groups. Designate an area in the room for each passion to meet. After all ones, twos, threes, fours, fives, sixes, sevens, and eights are grouped together, ask them to discuss in their group what are the most important points to make about their passion as they share with others, as well as which of the exercises that appear at the end of their passion they think would be most valuable to complete to gain insights into that particular passion. (10–15 minutes)

Step 3: Create new "sharing" groups. Each sharing group should have eight people total, and include one person from each expert group. If the number of participants you are working with is not divisible equally by eight, two people from a passion can present to their sharing group together. What is most important is that each newly formed sharing group contains at least one person that can represent each passion. (5 minutes)

Step 4: Once the new sharing groups are in place, designate a timekeeper in each group. The timekeeper gives each member of the group five minutes to share information about his or her passion based on the reading and their expert group discussion. (40 minutes)

Step 5: Facilitator leads a whole-group discussion by beginning with the question, "What have you learned about wondering development through engagement in this activity?" (15 minutes)

● *Activity 2.3: Passions Protocol*

This activity was developed based on Chapter 2 of our book by National School Reform Faculty members Pete Bermudez and Linda Emm. This activity, as well as other tips for helping teachers develop a wondering, appear in our companion book to this text, The Reflective Educator's Guide to Professional Development: Coaching Inquiry-Oriented Learning Communities, *also published by Corwin Press.*

Time: 60 minutes
Materials: Handout 3: Passion Profiles, paper or teachers' personal journals to write reflections, newsprint, markers

Directions:

Step 1: Read the passion profiles and identify the passion that most accurately describes who you are as an educator. If several fit (this will be true for many of you), choose the one that affects you the most, or the one that seems most significant as you reflect on your practice over time. (5 minutes)

Step 2: Without using the number of the passion profile, ask your colleagues questions and find the people who chose the same profile you did. (5 minutes)

Directions for Small Groups:

Step 1: Choose a facilitator/timer and a recorder/reporter.

Step 2: Check to see if you all really share that passion. Then, talk about your school experiences together. What is it like to have this passion—to be this kind of educator? Each person in the group should have an opportunity to talk, uninterrupted, for 2 minutes. (10 minutes)

Step 3: Next, each person in the group privately identifies an actual student, by name, who has been affected by the group's profile. Write in your journal (5 minutes):
- What have I done with this student?
- What's worked? What hasn't?
- What else could I do?
- What questions does this raise for me?

Step 4: Talk as a group about the questions that teachers who share this passion are likely to have about their practice. List as many of these questions as you can. (15 minutes)

The recorder/reporter should write on the newsprint, and should be ready to report out succinctly to the large group. Be sure to put your passion profile number at the top of the newsprint page.

Step 5: Whole-group debrief (after hearing from each passion profile group) (15 minutes):
- What strikes you as you listen to the passions of these educators? Listen for the silences. Where are they, and what do you make of them?
- Which of the questions generated intrigues you the most? Why? How might you go about exploring this question with colleagues? What would you do first?

Journal Writing Prompt

As you read Chapter 2 of *The Reflective Educator's Guide to Classroom Research* (Second Edition), use your journal to complete at least one exercise for each of the eight passions. The exercises are listed in shaded boxes after each passion is discussed in the chapter.

Resources for Extending Your Learning

Hubbard, R. S., & Power, B. M. (1999). *Living the questions: A guide for teacher researchers.* York, ME: Stenhouse.

Chapter 3. To Collaborate or Not to Collaborate: That Is the Question!

Summary

This chapter provides four reasons why teacher-inquirers should collaborate with others:

1. Research is hard work!
2. Teacher talk is important!
3. There's safety in numbers! and
4. There's strength in numbers!

In addition to establishing the critical importance of collaboration, this chapter offers four structures for veteran and/or beginning teachers to partner in inquiry. The first structure is termed "shared inquiry." Shared inquiry occurs when two or more practicing teachers, two or more prospective teachers, or a prospective and a practicing teacher pair or group define and conduct a single teacher research project together. The second structure is termed "parallel inquiry." Parallel inquiry occurs when teacher pairs (prospective teacher pairs, practicing teacher pairs, or a prospective and a practicing teacher pair) conduct two parallel but individual teacher research projects, working collectively to support each other's individual endeavors. The third structure is termed "intersecting inquiry." Intersecting inquiry occurs at times when teachers engage in individual inquiry projects that focus on the same topic, but explore different questions and wonderings about that topic. The final structure for collaboration is termed "inquiry support." Inquiry support occurs when prospective or practicing teacher-inquirers take full ownership of their inquiry project but invite one or more professionals who are not currently engaging in inquiry to support their work.

Discussion Questions

1. The authors state, "While we believe it is critical to make teacher inquiry *a part of* your teaching rather than *apart from* your teaching,

the fact remains that even if you are able to seamlessly integrate teaching and inquiry (as we believe should be the case!), the work is difficult and can be quite draining at times. Through collaboration with others, teacher-inquirers find a crucial source of energy and support that keeps them going and sustains their work." What are some ways you can make teacher inquiry *a part of* rather than *apart from* your teaching? How does working collaboratively with other educators generate energy?

2. Consider the following profiles of two teachers—"Always Collaborating Annie" and "Go It Alone Gail."

"Always Collaborating Annie" constantly seeks out others to give her feedback on and provide insights into her teaching. In fact, she does not feel confident teaching a lesson if she hasn't "run it by" at least one other colleague formally or informally to garner ideas and "test out" her lesson plan by describing it aloud. Rarely does Annie ever take any actions in her teaching without utilizing her colleagues as sounding boards for any changes to practice she is considering.

"Go It Alone Gail" rarely takes the opportunity to discuss her teaching with colleagues. Because she often eats lunch with students, she is rarely found in the teacher's room, so she has few opportunities to engage in professional dialogue with others during the school day. Because she coaches the girls' cross-country team and rushes to practice right after the final bell, she has few opportunities to engage in professional dialogue with others after school. Although the idea of collaboration appeals to Gail theoretically, she secretly admits to herself that she is glad her busy schedule precludes her from discussions with colleagues, as she is very action oriented and likes her teaching to keep moving in new directions. She could easily see herself getting frustrated by collaboration because it requires consensus and agreement and could potentially slow any changes to teaching practice that she is considering.

Are you more like "Always Collaborating Annie" or "Go It Alone Gail"? What implications do the ways you describe yourself as a collaborator have for your engagement in teacher inquiry?

3. What are some ways to create a culture of collaboration among teachers?

Activities

● *Activity 3.1: Four Corners*

Time: 30 minutes
Materials: Chart paper, masking tape, markers

Step 1: Using chart paper, create four posters by writing the letters "SA," "A," "D," and "SD" in large print. Hang each of the four posters in a different corner of the room.

Step 2: Point out the posters to participants. Tell participants that each corner of the room represents how you feel in relationship to a statement about collaboration that you are going to read. The corner labeled "SA" means you "strongly agree" with the statement. The corner labeled "A" means you "agree" with the statement. The corner labeled "D" means you "disagree" with the statement. The corner labeled "SD" means you "strongly disagree" with the statement.

Step 3: Read the following statement: "There is nothing more important than collaboration when it comes to teaching and inquiry." After you read the statement, ask participants to move to the corner that represents how they feel in relationship to the statement. After all participants have moved physically to one of the four corners, ask them to share with a person standing next to them why they placed themselves in that corner.

Step 4: After pairs share, facilitate a whole-group discussion by asking someone from each corner to share how he or she feels about the statement, "There is nothing more important than collaboration when it comes to teaching and inquiry." Make connections between what is shared in relationship to each statement to the content of Chapter 3, To Collaborate or Not to Collaborate: That Is the Question!

Step 5: Repeat Steps 3 and 4 with the following statements:
- In schools, it is impossible for teachers to find the time it takes to collaborate in meaningful ways.
- The profession of teaching will never change for the better unless teachers collaborate with one another.
- I feel comfortable with taking on the role of teacher leader and leading change based on what I learn as a result of my inquiry.
- I would rather engage in shared inquiry with a colleague than in parallel or intersecting inquiry.
- I would feel comfortable inviting a colleague to support my individual inquiry effort.
- I believe that the hard work of teaching and teacher research will be worth it!

Journal Writing Prompt

Which of the four structures for collaboration (shared inquiry, parallel inquiry, intersecting inquiry, or inquiry support) do you feel is *most* pertinent for you at this time in your professional lifetime? Why?

Chapter 4. Developing a Research Plan: Making Inquiry a Part of Your Teaching Practice

Summary

This chapter presents one dozen common strategies teacher-researchers use for capturing data in their classrooms and schools. These strategies are:

1. Fieldnotes
2. Documents/artifacts/student work
3. Interviews
4. Focus groups
5. Digital pictures
6. Video
7. Reflective journals
8. Weblogs
9. Surveys
10. Quantitative measures of student achievement (standardized test scores, assessment measures, grades)
11. Critical friend group feedback
12. Literature as data

(*Note to facilitator:* Chapter 7 provides a discussion of quality teacher research as well as presents a series of indicators that can strengthen the teacher-researcher's ability to develop an inquiry brief. We encourage you to read pages 175–176 of Chapter 7 that relate to developing an inquiry plan as you explore Chapter 4.)

Discussion Questions

1. Which teacher-researcher data collection strategies do you think are the easiest to incorporate into your teaching?
2. Which teacher-researcher data collection strategies do you think are the most difficult to incorporate into your teaching? How might these strategies be adapted so they fit better into the teaching day?
3. One strategy for taking fieldnotes includes inviting a teaching colleague to come into your classroom during his or her scheduled special or planning period to take notes for you. How comfortable do you feel having a colleague observe your teaching? What types of ground rules for peer observation would need to be in place to increase your comfort zone?
4. In what ways might your principal (if you are a practicing teacher) or university supervisor (if you are a prospective teacher) support your efforts to collect data?

5. The authors state, "Good teacher research is about more than generating good test scores or showing the relationship between one's teaching practice and one's students' performance on state tests." Do you agree or disagree with this statement? How can a teacher-researcher balance today's emphasis on standardized test scores with other sources of data when designing his or her inquiry?

6. How could the contents of Chapter 7 strengthen our ability to engage in developing an inquiry plan?

Activities

● *Activity 4.1: Open-Ended Sentences*

Time: 45–60 minutes

Materials: Handout 4: Seven Sentences That Capture How I Feel About Data Collection and Designing My Inquiry, newsprint, markers

Step 1: After reading Chapter 4, ask participants to complete Handout 4: Seven Sentences That Capture How I Feel About Data Collection and Designing My Inquiry. (10–15 minutes)

Step 2: Break into groups of four. In round-robin fashion, each member of the group shares one of their completed sentences with group members. Repeat this procedure three more times so that each member of the group has shared all of his or her completed sentences with group members. As each person shares one of his or her completed sentences, there is no comment or discussion. Rather, each person states one selected sentence, followed by the second person in the group, the third person, and finally, the fourth person. (10 minutes)

Step 3: After seven rounds of sharing, group members discuss common themes that they noticed across all their statements, jotting these themes on chart paper to report out to the whole group. (10 minutes)

Step 4: Ask each group to designate a "reporter" and allot each reporter a specified amount of time to share his or her group's themes with the entire group. The amount of time you spend on this step is dependent upon the number of groups you are working with. (approximately 15 minutes)

Step 5: Debrief the experience around the question, "What implications does what we learned about our feelings regarding data collection have for inquiry design?"

● *Activity 4.2: Inquiry Brief Feedback*

Time: Variable depending upon how many people are assigned to a group

Materials: Handout 5: Inquiry Brief Tuning Protocol—Six Steps to a Fine-Tuned Plan for Inquiry, enough copies of each individual's inquiry brief for each group member

Preparation: Participants bring with them copies of their own inquiry briefs created using the sample inquiry brief that appears at the end of Chapter 4.

Step 1: Review each step in the Inquiry Brief Discussion Protocol in Handout 5.

Step 2: Have participants form groups of three or four people each. Instruct them to follow the steps of the protocol for each member of their group to ensure that each group member receives valuable feedback.

Journal Writing Prompts

State the wondering you selected or are considering for your inquiry. Brainstorm a list of all the potential sources of data you can think of that would give you insights into this wondering. You may wish to return to Chapter 4 of *The Reflective Educator's Guide to Classroom Research* for a variety of data collection ideas. As you construct your list, think big—the sky's the limit! Once you have completed your list, discuss the most practical and least practical strategies on your list. What makes practical strategies practical and impractical strategies impractical? Are there any strategies on your list that you categorized as impractical that you believe could potentially provide valuable insights into your wondering? How might these impractical but valuable data collection tools be adapted to become more reasonable ways to collect data?

In the spirit of journal writing, read Julie Russell's journal entry that appears in Figure 4.9 in Chapter 4. In addition, skip ahead to Chapter 5 and read the excerpt from teacher-researcher Amy Ruth's journal that appears in Figure 5.3. What do you learn about the art of keeping a journal entry from reading these two real, live entries? Do you think keeping a reflective journal is a strategy you will employ when you complete your own inquiry? Why or why not?

Resources for Extending Your Learning

Creighton, T. B. (2007). *Schools and data: The educator's guide for using data to improve decision making.* Thousand Oaks, CA: Corwin Press.

Glesne, C. (2005). *Becoming qualitative researchers: An introduction* (Third Edition). New York: Longman.

Gregory, G. H., & Kuzmich, L. (2004). *Data driven differentiation in the standards-based classroom.* Thousand Oaks, CA: Corwin Press.

Janesick, V. J. (2003). *Stretching exercises for qualitative researchers.* Thousand Oaks, CA: Sage.

Chapter 5. Finding Your Findings: Data Analysis

Summary

This chapter helps the teacher-inquirers whom you work with understand the process of data analysis. The chapter begins by identifying data analysis as a systematic process that requires a great deal of data reduction as teacher-researchers sort through mounds of data that they have collected over the course of an inquiry. Following this brief overview, the analysis process is demystified as the reader is asked to recall Chapter 1's discussion of the competing research paradigms and remember that, although data analysis techniques are drawn from the field of social science, teacher-researchers use analysis techniques that are consonant with a teacher's life. This discussion reminds the reader that their prior conceptions of what research is—"number crunching" versus "storytelling"—can often make the data analysis process more difficult and uncertain.

Next, the chapter uses the metaphor of a jigsaw puzzle enthusiast to illustrate the data analysis process and then helps the reader understand the four-step process teacher-inquirers often use as they analyze their data—description, sense making, interpretation, and implication drawing. The description phase relies on the teacher-researcher simply describing what he or she saw as he or she inquired. After completing this phase, the teacher-researcher begins the sense-making process, which consists of highlighting the most important data nuggets and organizing the data in a way that fits together or "makes sense" to the teacher. Table 5.1 provides an overview of some ways that researchers have organized their data. After sense making, the researcher enters the interpretive phase of data analysis. This phase requires the teacher-researcher to construct statements that express what was learned, as well as what this learning means for future teaching practice. In this phase, teacher-researchers typically look back at their initial wondering in light of the emerging patterns identified in the analysis and use them to illustrate, organize, and communicate the inquiry findings to others. Table 5.2 offers a summary of some strategies that teacher-researchers often find useful in the interpretive phase.

Given that the goal of inquiry is to improve practice, teacher-researchers are expected to take a final step in analysis to draw implications that would improve practice. This phase requires the teacher-researcher to make public the consequences, changes, and future questions that have emerged from the inquiry.

After describing the four-step process, Chapter 5 provides an example of what data analysis might look like by introducing the reader to Amy Ruth, a veteran teacher-researcher. Amy shares the process that she used to analyze three different types of data.

(*Note to facilitator:* Facilitators should consider having their participants read pages 176–178 of Chapter 7, which focuses on assessing the quality of findings in teacher research, at the same time as they read Chapter 5. By using both chapters together, the inquiry analysis process can be strengthened.)

Discussion Questions

1. How does jargon or technical language, as well as our own prior conceptions about educational research and the uncertainness of the inductive process, complicate teacher inquiry?
2. How does the jigsaw puzzle enthusiast metaphor connect to the data analysis process? What other metaphors might characterize this process?
3. What steps of the analysis process appear most complex and why?
4. In what ways are the purposes of Table 5.1 and Table 5.2 different?
5. Review each of the figures presented in Chapter 5. What tips do they offer about engaging in the analysis process?
6. As we engage in the data analysis process, how might we use each other to strengthen our work?
7. How could we use Chapter 7 to strengthen our ability to engage in data analysis?

Activities

● *Activity 5.1: Data Analysis Summary*
   Sheet and Data Analysis Protocol

This activity is designed to help inquirers move through the data analysis process and receive support from their colleagues. The data analysis summary sheet is completed independently and the data analysis protocol is a tool used by teachers working together to strengthen the analysis effort.

Time: 30 minutes to complete Handout 6: Data Analysis Summary Sheet, 90 minutes for a group of three to complete data analysis protocol
Materials: Handout 6: Data Analysis Summary Sheet, data analysis protocol, pencils

Data Analysis Summary Sheet

Part 1: Give the participants in your group time to complete Handout 6: Data Analysis Summary Sheet questions. This can be done within the work session, but we often find that it's best if participants complete the Data Analysis Summary Sheet prior to coming to the session.

Part 2: After completing the summary sheet, organize the participants in groups of three. Think carefully about the group membership. For example, you might want to group inquirers together based on topic, or you may want to group inquirers by grade level. Participants often have strong feelings about what grouping strategy would be most beneficial to them, so be sure to include them in the grouping decision. Engage in the "Data Analysis Protocol."

Data Analysis Protocol

Step 1: Presenter shares his or her inquiry (4 minutes). Presenter briefly shares with his or her group members the focus/purpose of his or her inquiry, what his or her wonderings were, how data were collected, and the initial sense that the presenter has made of his or her data. Completing the following sentences prior to discussion may help presenter organize his or her thoughts prior to sharing:

- The issue/tension/dilemma/problem/interest that led me to my inquiry was . . .
- Therefore, the purpose of my inquiry was to . . .
- My wondering(s) was . . .
- I collected data by . . .
- So far, three discoveries I've made from reading through my data are . . .

Step 2: Group members ask clarifying questions (3 minutes). Group members ask questions that have factual answers to clarify their understanding of the inquiry, such as, "How long did you collect data for?" "How many students did you work with?"

Step 3: The group asks probing questions of the presenter (7 minutes). The group members then ask probing questions. These questions are worded so that they help the presenter clarify and expand his or her thinking about what he or she is learning from the data. During this 10-minute time frame, the presenter may respond to the group's questions, but there is no discussion by the group of the presenter's responses. Every member of the group should pose at least one question of the presenter. Some examples of probing questions might include:

a. What are some ways you might organize your data? (See Table 5.1 in *The Reflective Educator's Guide to Classroom Research.*)

b. What might be some powerful ways to present your data? (See Table 5.2 in *The Reflective Educator's Guide to Classroom Research.*)

c. Do you have any data that doesn't seem to "fit"?
d. Based on your data, what are you learning about yourself as a teacher?
e. What is your data telling you about the students you teach?
f. What are the implications of your findings for the content you teach?
g. What have you learned about the larger context of schools and schooling?
h. What are the implications of what you have learned for your teaching?
i. What changes might you make in your own practice?
j. What new wonderings do you have?

Step 4: Group members discuss the data analysis (6 minutes). The group talks with each other about the data analysis presented, discussing such questions as, "What did we hear?" "What didn't we hear that we think might be relevant?" "What assumptions seem to be operating?" "Does any data not seem to fit with the presenter's analysis?" "What might be some additional ways to look at the presenter's data?" During this discussion, members of the group work to deepen the data analysis. Participants can draw on the discussion of quality indicators presented in Chapter 7 to strengthen the discussion and the findings. The presenter doesn't speak during this discussion, but instead listens and takes notes.

Step 5: Presenter reflection (3 minutes). The presenter reflects on what he or she heard and what he or she is now thinking, sharing with the group anything that particularly resonated for him or her during any part of the group members' data analysis discussion.

Step 6: Reflection on the process (2 minutes). Group shares thoughts about how the discussion worked for the group.

Journal Writing Prompt

After reading Chapter 5 of *The Reflective Educator's Guide to Classroom Research* (Second Edition), use your journal to complete Exercises 1 through 4. The exercises are listed in shaded boxes at the end of the chapter.

Resources for Extending Your Learning

The following books also include overviews of the data analysis process.

Anderson, G. L., Herr, K. G., & Nihlen, A. S. (1994). *Studying your own school: An educator's guide to qualitative practitioner research.* Thousand Oaks, CA: Corwin Press.

Hubbard, R. S., & Power, B. M. (1999). *Living the questions: A guide for teacher researchers.* York, ME: Stenhouse.

Mills, G. (2006). *Action research: A guide for the teacher researcher* (Third Edition). Englewood Cliffs, NJ: Prentice Hall.

Sagor, R. (2004). *The action research guidebook: A four-step process for educators and school teams.* Thousand Oaks, CA: Corwin Press.

Chapter 6. Extending Your Learning: The Inquiry Write-Up

Summary

This chapter begins by emphasizing how writing can extend the analysis process by helping a teacher clarify his or her thinking about the inquiry. As a result, we explore four compelling reasons to write up the inquiry, including clarification, empowerment, generativity, and accomplishment. After heightening the importance of the writing process, the rest of the chapter shares an example of Julie Russell's inquiry write-up by taking the reader step-by-step through the stages of providing background information, sharing the design of the inquiry, stating the learning and supporting the statements with data, and providing concluding thoughts.

(*Note to facilitator:* Facilitators should consider having their participants review Chapter 7, which focuses on assessing the quality of teacher research, at the same time as they read this chapter. By using both chapters together, the inquiry "writing it up" process can be strengthened.)

Discussion Questions

1. How might writing deepen the analysis process? Why is writing important?
2. When might teacher-researchers carve out time to write up their inquiries?
3. Which of the four steps of the inquiry write-up do you feel most comfortable completing and why?
4. What does it mean to support a statement with data?
5. After reading the example in the chapter, discuss the techniques that Julie Russell used to support her findings with evidence. Why was this evidence so important in writing up her inquiry?
6. What would you have liked to see in Julie Russell's inquiry write-up that was not present?

7. What are some other alternatives to writing up an inquiry, and if these other alternatives were used in place of the inquiry write-up, how would you be sure that the teacher-researcher attended to each of the four steps?
8. How could Chapter 7 strengthen our ability to write up our inquiry?

Activities

• *Activity 6.1: Writer's Workshop*

This activity introduces the writer's workshop process as a vehicle that creates a community of support for teacher-inquirers as they engage in "writing it up." As the facilitator, you will need to help your group identify two 90-minute sessions to work on "writing it up" using the workshop process (prewrite, write, edit, revise, conference, publish). Teachers will also need to identify about 4 hours of time to independently write drafts for review. It is important that this writing time is blocked out and protected to allow teachers the opportunity to brainstorm, write drafts, edit and proofread each other's work, then publish their inquiries. Given the time-intensive nature of teaching, teachers will benefit by having these timelines for their writing.

Time: Two 90-minute sessions
Materials: Drafts, pencils, paper

Step 1: Teachers outline their inquiry write-ups and share with a peer partner or facilitator.

Step 2: Teachers write their drafts.

Step 3: Teachers edit and proofread each other's write-ups. Probe using the quality indicators from Chapter 7.

Step 4: Teachers create the final drafts of their inquiry write-ups.

Journal Writing Prompt

After reading Chapter 6 of *The Reflective Educator's Guide to Classroom Research* (Second Edition), use your journal to outline an inquiry write-up for your study using the four components of a write-up shared in the chapter:

1. Providing background information
2. Sharing the design of the inquiry (procedures, data collection, and data analysis)
3. Stating the learning and supporting the statements with data
4. Providing concluding thoughts

Resources for Extending Your Learning

The following books and resources provide examples of additional teacher research write-ups and writer's workshop as a professional development tool:

Caro-Bruce, C., Flessner, R., Klehr, M., & Zeichner, K. M. (2007). *Creating equitable classrooms through action research.* Thousand Oaks, CA: Corwin Press.

Lieberman, A., & Wood, D. R. (2002). *Inside the National Writing Project: Connecting network learning and classroom teaching.* New York: Teachers College Press.

Chapter 7. Becoming the Best Teacher and Researcher You Can Be: Assessing the Quality of Your Own and Others' Inquiry

Summary

The first section of the chapter differentiates between the ideas of generalizability and transferability, identifies the complexity created as a result of teacher inquiry having multiple goals, and raises numerous reasons that make assessing teacher inquiry difficult. The second section of the chapter offers five quality indicators that teacher-inquirers can utilize to assess the quality of their own work. Each indicator includes many questions that help prompt self-assessment. The chapter concludes by emphasizing the importance of having an experienced coach to serve as a critical friend interested in deepening both the process and the knowledge constructed.

Given that Chapter 7 focuses on teaching the inquirer how to assess the quality of his or her own inquiry, the information presented in this chapter can help the teacher-researcher in all phases of the inquiry process, from conceptualization to generating findings to writing up the inquiry. Facilitators can use parts of this chapter in conjunction with Chapters 2, 4, 5, and 6 to deepen participants' understandings of how to enhance the quality of a wondering, data collection, data analysis, and writing up the inquiry, respectively.

Discussion Questions

1. Why is it important to assess the quality of teacher research?
2. How is teacher research a tool for both professional development and contributing to the knowledge base of teaching? Is one of these goals more important to you at this time? Why or why not?

3. Why is it difficult to assess the quality of teacher research?
4. What is the difference between generalizability and transferability?
5. What are the quality indicators for teacher research? How can we use these to strengthen our teacher research?
6. Which indicators present the greatest challenges to novice researchers? Why?
7. How can this chapter be used to deepen the work we completed in conjunction with Chapters 2, 4, 5, and 6?

Activities

● *Activity 7.1: The Four A's Protocol: Understanding the Complexity of Assessing Teacher Inquiry*

This activity was modified from a protocol titled "Four A's Text," adapted by Judith Gray of Seattle, Washington, from the National School Reform Faculty Web site. Please visit their Web site (www.nsrfharmony.org) for additional text-based protocols that can be utilized to discuss this chapter.

Time: 25 minutes
Materials: Handout 7: Four A's Protocol, participant-selected significant ideas (Four A's) from Chapter 7; timer

Step 1: Organize participants in groups of four to five.

Step 2: Before the meeting, ask participants to read the chapter and write notes in the margin, on Post-it notes, or on Handout 7 to answer the following four questions:
- What do you agree with in the text?
- What do you argue with in the text?
- What assumptions are the authors making about you and the inquiry process in the text?
- What parts of the text do you want to aspire to?

Step 3: Each person in the group takes a turn sharing an assumption in the text, pointing out the location and evidence for their thinking.

Step 4: Continue this process by inviting each person to share their ideas relating to each of the remaining Four A's.

Step 5: End the session by asking participants what they have learned about striving for quality in teacher research.

● *Activity 7.2: Strengthening the Inquiry Brief, Inquiry Analysis Protocol, and Writing It Up Process*

In place of, or in addition to leading the group through Activity 7.1, the facilitator could elect to integrate the contents of Chapter 7 into the activities completed in Chapters 2, 4, 5, and 6. We believe that by looking at the quality indicators as teacher-inquirers are designing and engaging in the inquiry process, teacher research can be strengthened. For example, the quality indicators related to wondering development could be discussed after reading Chapter 2.

We suggest that when working on:

- Chapter 2, participants read pages 165–175 to help them strengthen their wonderings (with a particular focus on Quality Indicator #2, pages 174–175).
- Chapter 4, participants read pages 175–176 (Quality Indicator #3) to help them create a powerful inquiry plan.
- Chapter 5, participants read pages 176–178 (Quality Indicators #4 and 5) to help them with their analysis.
- Chapter 6, participants review all of the quality indicators (pages 173–178) to help them with writing up their work.

The quality indicators shared in this chapter can serve as probes and prompts to be used by the inquirers themselves or by critical friends committed to helping their colleagues through the inquiry process.

Journal Writing Prompts

In your journal, discuss how you have attended to the quality indicators shared in this chapter. Identify what the strengths and weaknesses of your study might be and how you might respond to these strengths and weaknesses in your future inquiries.

In your journal, explore how you and your colleagues could create a mechanism for providing honest feedback to each other that both honors and celebrates your work to date but also provides areas for future growth and development as teacher-researchers.

Chapter 8. The End of Your Journey: Making Your Inquiry Public

Summary

This chapter explores how teacher-inquirers can make their inquiries public to other educators and discusses why sharing their work is an important component to the inquiry process. After highlighting the importance of making inquiry work public, Chapter 8 introduces a variety of structures such as study groups, journals, poster sessions, Web sites, faculty meetings, national networks, and conferences.

Discussion Questions

1. What structures might be possible for sharing inquiry within our context? What would be the strengths and weaknesses of

each of these options? What would it take to make an inquiry sharing occur in our context?

2. How might we include our colleagues who are not engaged in inquiry into our work and generate their interest in inquiry?

3. How might we capture what we learn from our collective inquiries so that others can benefit from our work?

Activities

● *Activity 8.1: Chalk Talk*

This activity was based on the protocol titled "Chalk Talk," originally developed by Hildon Smith, Foxfire Fund, and adapted for the National School Reform Faculty by Marilyn Wentworth. It is a silent way to generate ideas about how your group might share their inquiry work. Please visit NSRF's Web site (www.nsrfharmony.org) for additional protocols that can be utilized to discuss this chapter.

Time: 15 minutes
Materials: Chalkboard or paper roll, markers

Step 1: Explain to the group members that a Chalk Talk is a silent activity. You can comment on other people's ideas by drawing a connecting line from your idea to someone else's comment.

Step 2: Write on the board, "How can we share our work with our colleagues?" and "Who would benefit from hearing about our work?"

Step 3: Participants write their ideas on the chalkboard. There will probably be long, natural silences.

Step 4: The facilitator can join the group by writing probing comments.

Step 5: After the 15 minutes has ended, bring the group together. Engage the group in a conversation about what strategies might work in your context. Develop an action plan for making your inquiry group's work public.

Journal Writing Prompt

Describe how you would (or did) feel about sharing your inquiry with others. What are (or were) you concerned about prior to sharing? What could (or did) the process do for you? What could (or did) the sharing process do for others?

Handouts

Handout 1: Twelve Interesting Quotes From Chapter 1

Directions: Copy and cut apart so each member of your group receives one quote.

Teacher inquiry is a vehicle that can be used by teachers to untangle some of the complexities that occur in the profession, raise teachers' voices in discussions of educational reform, and ultimately transform assumptions about the teaching profession itself.	Given today's political context, where much of the decision making and discussion regarding teachers occur outside the walls of the classroom (Darling-Hammond, 1994; Cochran-Smith & Lytle, 2006), the time seems ripe to create a movement where teachers are armed with the tools of inquiry and committed to educational change.
While both the process-product and qualitative research paradigms have generated valuable insights into the teaching and learning process, they have not included the voices of the people closest to the children—classroom teachers. Hence, a third research tradition emerges highlighting the role classroom teachers play as knowledge generators. This tradition is often referred to as "teacher research," "teacher inquiry," "classroom research," "action research," or "practitioner inquiry."	In general, the teacher inquiry movement focuses on the concerns of teachers (not outside researchers) and engages teachers in the design, data collection, and interpretation of data around a question. Termed "action research" by Carr and Kemmis (1986), this approach to educational research has many benefits: (1) Theories and knowledge are generated from research grounded in the realities of educational practice, (2) teachers become collaborators in educational research by investigating their own problems, and (3) teachers play a part in the research process, which makes them more likely to facilitate change based on the knowledge they create.
Very simply put, inquiry is a way for me to continue growing as a teacher. Before I became involved in inquiry I'd gotten to the point where I'd go to an inservice and shut off my brain. Most of the teachers I know have been at the same place. If you have been around at all you know that most inservices are the same cheese—just repackaged. Inquiry lets me choose my own growth and gives me tools to validate or jettison my ideas. (Kreinbihl, 2007)	You know that nagging that wakes you in the early hours, then reemerges during your morning preparation time so you cannot remember if you already applied the deodorant, later on the drive to school pushing out of mind those important tasks you needed to accomplish prior to the first bell, and again as the students are entering your class and sharing all the important things happening in their lives. Well, teacher inquiry is the formal stating of that nagging, developing a plan of action to do something about it, putting the plan into action, collecting data, analyzing the collected works, making meaning of your collection, sharing your findings, then repeating the cycle with the new nagging(s) that sprouted up. (Hughes, 2007)

(Continued)

(Continued)

Teacher inquiry is not something I do; it is more a part of the way I think. Inquiry involves exciting and meaningful discussions with colleagues about the passions we embrace in our profession. It has become the gratifying response to formalizing the questions that enter my mind as I teach. It is a learning process that keeps me passionate about teaching. (Hubbell, 2007)	Teacher inquiry differs from traditional professional development for teachers, which has typically focused on the knowledge of an outside "expert" being shared with a group of teachers. This traditional model of professional growth, usually delivered as a part of traditional staff development, may appear an efficient method of disseminating information but often does not result in real and meaningful change in the classroom.
This movement toward a new model of professional growth based on inquiry into one's own practice can be powerfully developed by school districts and building administrators as a form of professional development. By participating in teacher inquiry, the teacher develops a sense of ownership in the knowledge constructed, and this sense of ownership heavily contributes to the possibilities for real change to take place in the classroom.	By cultivating this inquiry stance toward teaching, teachers play a critical role in enhancing their own professional growth and, ultimately, the experience of schooling for children. Thus, an inquiry stance is synonymous with professional growth and provides a nontraditional approach to staff development that can lead to meaningful change for children.
Action research is a wonderful tool teachers can utilize to differentiate instruction, ultimately making schools a better place for all students, regardless of their interests, abilities, background, and learning styles.	By embracing an inquiry approach, teachers expand their idea of what data is and how using data can inform their teaching and enhance student learning. The inquiry stance embraced by teacher-researchers supports both data-driven decision making and progress monitoring.

Handout 2: The Great Wondering Brainstorm

Directions: As you read Chapter 2 in *The Reflective Educator's Guide to Classroom Research,* brainstorm one to three "wonderings" in each category.

A Child _____

_____

_____

_____

_____

Curriculum _____

_____

_____

_____

_____

Content Knowledge _____

_____

_____

_____

Teaching Strategies/Techniques _____

_____

_____

_____

(Continued)

(Continued)

Beliefs About Practice _____

_____

_____

_____

_____

Personal/Professional Identity _____

_____

_____

_____

_____

Social Justice _____

_____

_____

_____

_____

Context _____

_____

_____

_____

_____

Handout 3: Passion Profiles

*pas-sion n. 1. A powerful emotion, such as love, joy, hatred, or anger. 2. a. Ardent love.
3. a. Boundless enthusiasm . . .*

Passion 1: The Child

You became a teacher primarily because you wanted to make a difference in the life of a child. Perhaps you were one of those whose life was changed by a committed, caring teacher and you decided to become a teacher so that you could do that for other children. You are always curious about particular students whose work and/or behavior just doesn't seem to be in sync with the rest of the students in your class. You often wonder about how peer interactions seem to affect a student's likelihood to complete assignments, or what enabled one of your English language learning students to make such remarkable progress seemingly overnight, or how to motivate a particular student to get into the habit of writing. You believe that understanding the unique qualities that each student brings to your class is the key to unlocking all their full potential as learners.

Passion 2: The Curriculum

You are one of those teachers who are always "tinkering" with the curriculum to enrich the learning opportunities for your students. You have a thorough understanding of your content area. You attend conferences and subscribe to journals that help you to stay up on current trends affecting the curriculum that you teach. Although you are often dissatisfied with "what is" with respect to the prescribed curriculum in your school or district, you are almost always sure that you could do it better than the frameworks. You are always critiquing the existing curriculum and finding ways to make it better for the kids you teach—especially when you have a strong hunch that "there is a better way to do this."

Passion 3: Content Knowledge

You are at your best in the classroom when you have a thorough understanding of the content and/or topic you are teaching. Having to teach something you don't know much about makes you uncomfortable and always motivates you to hone up this area of your teaching knowledge base. You realize that what you know about what you are teaching will influence how you get it across to your students in a developmentally appropriate way. You spend a considerable amount of your personal time—both during the school year and in the summer—looking for books, material, workshops, and courses you can take that will strengthen your content knowledge.

Passion 4: Teaching Strategies

You are motivated most as a teacher by a desire to improve on and experiment with teaching strategies and techniques. You have experienced and understand the value of particular strategies to engage students in powerful learning and want to get really good at this stuff.

(Continued)

(Continued)

Although you have become really comfortable with using cooperative learning with your students, there are many other strategies and techniques that interest you and that you want to incorporate into your teaching repertoire.

Passion 5: The Relationship Between Beliefs and Professional Practice

You sense a disconnect between what you believe and what actually happens in your classroom and/or school. For example, you believe that a major purpose of schools is to produce citizens capable of contributing to and sustaining a democratic society; however, students in your class seldom get an opportunity to discuss controversial issues because you fear that the students you teach may not be ready and/or capable of this, and you are concerned about losing control of the class.

Passion 6: The Intersection Between Your Personal and Professional Identities

You came into teaching from a previous career and often sense that your previous identity may be in conflict with your new identity as an educator. You feel ineffective and frustrated when your students or colleagues don't approach a particular task that is second nature to you because of your previous identity—for example, writer, actor, artist, researcher—in the same way that you do. What keeps you up at night is how to use the knowledge, skills, and experiences you bring from your previous life to make powerful teaching and learning happen in your classroom and/or school.

Passion 7: Advocating Equity and Social Justice

You became an educator to change the world—to help create a more just, equitable, democratic, and peaceful planet. You are constantly thinking of ways to integrate issues of race, class, disability, power, and the like into your teaching; however, your global concerns for equity and social justice sometimes get in the way of your effectiveness as an educator—like the backlash that resulted from the time you showed *Schindler's List* to your sixth-grade class. You know there are more developmentally appropriate ways to infuse difficult and complex issues into your teaching and want to learn more about how to do this with your students.

Passion 8: Context Matters

What keeps you up at night is wondering how to keep students focused on learning despite the many disruptions that go on in your classroom or building on a daily basis. It seems that the school context conspires against everything that you know about teaching and learning—adults who don't model the behaviors they want to see reflected in the students, policies that are in conflict with the school's mission, and above all a high-stakes testing environment that tends to restrain the kind of teaching and learning that you know really works for the students you teach.

Handout 4: Seven Sentences That Capture How I Feel About Data Collection and Designing My Inquiry

Directions: In Chapter 4 of *The Reflective Educator's Guide to Classroom Research*, 12 data collection strategies for teacher-researchers are described:

1. Fieldnotes
2. Documents/artifacts/ student work
3. Interviews
4. Focus groups
5. Digital pictures
6. Video
7. Reflective journals
8. Weblogs
9. Surveys
10. Quantitative measures of student achievement (standardized test scores, assessment measures, grades)
11. Critical friend group feedback
12. Literature

Complete the following sentences in relationship to these data collection strategies.

1. One word that captures how I feel about all these data collection strategies is _____. I chose this word because _____

_____

_____

_____

_____

2. I was surprised that _____ could be considered a form of data!

3. The easiest data collection strategy for me to use as a teacher-researcher would be

_____ because _____

_____

_____

_____

_____

(Continued)

(Continued)

4. The most difficult data collection strategy for me to use as a teacher-researcher is

_____ because _____

_____

_____

_____

_____

5. The thing I find most interesting about data collection for the teacher-researcher is

_____

_____

_____

_____

6. One thing that puzzles me about data collection for the teacher-researcher is _____

_____

_____

_____

_____

7. As I design my first inquiry, I will be sure to _____

_____

_____

_____

_____

Handout 5: Inquiry Brief Tuning Protocol— Six Steps to a Fine-Tuned Plan for Inquiry

Suggested Group Size: Three or four

Suggested Time Frame: 15–20 minutes per group member

Step 1: Select a timekeeper.

Step 2: Presenter hands out a hard copy of the inquiry brief to each member of the group.

Step 3: Group members silently read the inquiry brief, making notes of issues/questions they might like to raise in discussion with presenter. (4 minutes)

As group members read the brief, presenter engages in a writing activity to complete the following sentences:
- Something I would like help with on my inquiry brief is . . .
- One thing this group needs to know about me or my proposed inquiry to better prepare them to assist me is . . .

Step 4: At the end of 4 minutes (or when it is clear that every member of the group has completed reading and taking notes on the inquiry brief, and the presenter has finished his or her response to the writing activity), the timekeeper invites the presenter to read his or her sentence completion activity out loud. (No more than 1 minute)

Step 5: Participants talk to each other as if the presenter was not in the room, while the presenter remains silent and takes notes. (10 minutes)

Participants focus on each of the following:
- Provide "warm feedback" on the inquiry brief. This is feedback that is positive in nature and identifies areas of strength. (1 or 2 minutes)
- Address the area the presenter would like help on and discuss the following questions: (8–10 minutes)
  a. What match seems to exist (or not exist) between the proposed data collection plan and inquiry question?
  b. Are there additional types of data that would give the participant insights into his or her question?
  c. Rate the doability of this plan for inquiry. In what ways is the participant's plan meshed with the everyday work of a teacher?
  d. In what ways does the participant's proposed timeline for study align with each step in the action research process?
  e. What possible disconnects and problems do you see?

Step 6: Timekeeper asks presenter to summarize the key points made during discussion that he or she wishes to consider in refining the plan for inquiry. (1 minute)

Handout 6: Data Analysis Summary Sheet

The issue/tension/dilemma/problem/interest that led me to my inquiry was _____

_____

_____

_____

_____

Therefore, the purpose of my inquiry was to _____

_____

_____

_____

_____

My wondering(s) was, "_____

_____

_____

_____

_____

_____"

I collected data by _____

_____

_____

_____

_____

_____

_____

So far, three discoveries I've made from reading through my data are:

1. _____

_____

_____

_____

_____

2. _____

_____

_____

_____

_____

3. _____

_____

_____

_____

_____

Handout 7: Four A's Protocol

A gree with	A rgue with
A ssumptions	**A** spire to

Other thoughts for discussion: _____

_____

_____

_____

_____

Sample Workshop Agendas

Half-Day Workshops, University Course Meetings, or Afterschool Meetings

If you are using this book to lead a group of teachers through a cycle of action research, or as a part of a university course focused on teachers' engagement in research where each student conducts inquiry as a course requirement, we believe the content of our book is most effectively covered by exploring each step in the teacher inquiry process (each chapter of the book) at specified intervals throughout the school year. In this way, the product of these workshops or course meetings becomes each participant's own teacher research.

In this section, we have included sample workshop agendas for workshops or meetings that are approximately 2–3 hours in length, as well as suggested activities for participants to complete between one meeting and the next. We have also provided a sample timeline for these workshops that spreads inquiry over the course of a school year, beginning in September and ending in May. This schedule can be adjusted to fit a typical 16-week semester course or other timeframe based on your needs and your context. In addition, each of these individual sessions can be lengthened or shortened depending upon the depth you wish to reach within each session, as well as how much activity you wish to assign between meetings.

Meeting 1: Introduction to Teacher Inquiry (September)

The purpose of this meeting is to provide an overview of the teacher inquiry process.

Welcome and Get Acquainted Activity (30 minutes)

Invite a Teacher-Researcher to Share a Recent Inquiry With the Group (60 minutes)

Activity 1.1: Block Party or Activity 1.2: Save the Last Word for Me (30 minutes)

In Preparation for Meeting 2: Developing Your Wondering

- Read Chapters 1 and 2 as well as review pages 174–175 (Quality Indicator #2) of *The Reflective Educator's Guide to Classroom Research* (Second Edition).
- *(Optional)* Complete one or more of the exercises that appear throughout Chapter 2 at the end of each passion. By engaging in these exercises, you begin the process of exploring one or more possible wonderings you wish to examine about your teaching practice.

Meeting 2: Developing Your Wondering (October)

The purpose of this meeting is to give each member of your group an opportunity to explore multiple possibilities for wonderings, as well as share and receive feedback on one or more proposed wondering(s). This meeting should be approached with the following mindset:

> Rarely does any teacher-researcher eloquently state his or her wondering immediately. It takes time, brainstorming, and actually "playing" with the question . . . By playing with the wording of a wondering, teachers often fine-tune and discover more detail about the subject they are really passionate about understanding. (Dana & Yendol-Hoppey, 2009, pp. 57–58))

Welcome and Overview of Meeting (10 minutes)

Activity 2.3: Passions Protocol (60 minutes)

Activity 2.1: The Great Wondering Brainstorm (30–45 minutes)

Form groups. Have each person share the wondering from "The Great Wondering Brainstorm" that he or she is most passionate about exploring this year. Have group members provide feedback. (30–60 minutes)

> ### *In Preparation for Meeting 3:*
> ### *Collaboration and Data Collection*
>
> - Read Chapters 3 and 4 as well as review pages 175–176 (Quality Indicator #3) of Chapter 7 of *The Reflective Educator's Guide to Classroom Research* (Second Edition).

Meeting 3: Collaboration and Data Collection (November)

The purpose of this meeting is to review two essential elements in the design of any inquiry: collaborative inquiry structures and data collection strategies.

Welcome and Overview of Meeting (15 minutes)

Activity 3.1: Four Corners (30 minutes)

Activity 4.1: Open-Ended Sentences (45 minutes)

Participants Begin to Write Their Own Personal Inquiry Brief (remaining time)

> ### *In Preparation for Meeting 4: Designing Your Inquiry*
>
> - Read Chapter 4 as well as review pages 173–178 of Chapter 7 of *The Reflective Educator's Guide to Classroom Research* (Second Edition).
> - Design an inquiry brief. (An example of a brief appears on pages 113–114 of the text.)
> - Bring copies of your inquiry brief to the next meeting (enough copies for each group member to have one).

Meeting 4: Designing Your Inquiry (December)

The purpose of this meeting is for each member of the group to give and receive feedback on each teacher's inquiry brief. A goal to strive for is to have each teacher leave this meeting with a fine-tuned plan (including a timeline) to conduct his or her inquiry.

Welcome and Overview of Meeting (15 minutes)

Activity 4.2: Inquiry Brief Feedback (60–120 minutes)

In Preparation for Meetings 5 and 6: Data Analysis

- Continue to collect data, including reading literature that will inform your inquiry.
- Read Chapter 5 as well as review pages 173–178 of Chapter 7 in *The Reflective Educator's Guide to Classroom Research* (Second Edition).
- Prior to your next meeting, read through the data you have collected so far and complete Handout 5 (Data Analysis Summary Sheet).

(*Note:* If your group has not decided how they will share their inquiries by this point, you might want to hold an additional meeting dedicated to processing Chapter 8 and determining the details related to how the inquiry will be made public.)

Meetings 5 and 6: Data Analysis (February and March)

The purpose of these meetings is for each member of the group to give and receive feedback on his or her analysis activities. A goal to strive for is to have each teacher leave this meeting with a stronger and more clarified understanding of his or her findings.

Welcome and Overview of Meeting (15 minutes)

Activity 5.1: Data Analysis Protocol (60–120 minutes)

In Preparation for Meetings 7 and 8: Writing It Up!

- Read Chapters 6 and 7 in *The Reflective Educator's Guide to Classroom Research* (Second Edition) and create an outline of your inquiry.

Meetings 7 and 8: Writing It Up (April)

The purpose of these two meetings, which need to occur close together within the same month, is to write up the inquiry. A writer's workshop approach can help the participants with the process of writing up the inquiry.

Welcome and Overview of Meeting (15 minutes)

Activity 6.1: Writer's Workshop (60–120 minutes)

> ### In Preparation for Meeting 9:
> ### Sharing Your Inquiry With Others
>
> - Read Chapter 8 in *The Reflective Educator's Guide to Classroom Research* (Second Edition). Complete your inquiry write-up and presentation materials.

Meeting 9: Sharing Your Inquiry With Others (May)

The purpose of this gathering is to celebrate the professional development that has occurred, the inquiry stance that has been cultivated, and the professional knowledge that has been constructed through inquiry. Congratulations!

(*Note:* Ideas for structuring a sharing session can be found in Chapter 6 of *The Reflective Educator's Guide to Professional Development: Coaching Inquiry-Oriented Learning Communities.*)

Workshop Evaluation Form

- How well did the seminar meet the goals and objectives?

- What professional support will you need to implement what you have learned from this seminar?

- How well did the topics explored in this seminar meet a specific need in your school or district?

- How relevant was this topic to your professional life?

Process

- How well did the instructional techniques and activities facilitate your understanding of the topic?

- How can you incorporate the activities learned today into your daily professional life?

- Was a variety of learning experiences included in the seminar?

- Was any particular activity memorable? What made it stand out?

Context

- Were the facilities conducive to learning?

- Were the accommodations adequate for the activities involved?

Overall

- Overall, how successful would you consider this seminar? Please include a brief comment or explanation.

- What was the most valuable thing you gained from this seminar experience?

Additional Comments

SOURCE: Adapted from *Evaluating Professional Development* by Thomas R. Guskey, Corwin Press, 2000.

Notes

CORWIN PRESS

The Corwin Press logo—a raven striding across an open book—represents the union of courage and learning. Corwin Press is committed to improving education for all learners by publishing books and other professional development resources for those serving the field of PreK–12 education. By providing practical, hands-on materials, Corwin Press continues to carry out the promise of its motto: **"Helping Educators Do Their Work Better."**